STAND UP   SPEAK OUT

PEACE ACTIVISM

Virginia Loh-Hagan

PEACE NOW!

MORE ♥ Love

1

45 45TH PARALLEL PRESS

Published in the United States of America by Cherry Lake Publishing Group
Ann Arbor, Michigan
www.cherrylakepublishing.com

Reading Adviser: Beth Walker Gambro, MS, Ed., Reading Consultant, Yorkville, IL
Book Designer: Jen Wahi

Photo Credits: © somkhana/Shutterstock.com, 4; © Johnny Silvercloud/Shutterstock.com, 6; © Scott Woodham
Photography/Shutterstock.com, 8; © Halfpoint/Shutterstock.com, 11; © Melih Cevdet Teksen/Shutterstock.com, 12;
© Romolo Tavani /Shutterstock.com, 14; © Dmitry Kalinovsky/Shutterstock.com, 17; © Everett Collection/Shutterstock.
com, 18; © Stuart Monk/Shutterstock.com, 20; © Blulz60/Shutterstock.com, 23; © Nelson Antoine/Shutterstock.com, 24;
© slobo/iStock.com, 26; © Leszek Glasner/Shutterstock.com, 29; © FG Trade/iStock.com, 30, additional cover images
courtesy of iStock.com

45th Parallel Press is an imprint of Cherry Lake Publishing Group.

Library of Congress Cataloging-in-Publication Data

Names: Loh-Hagan, Virginia, author.
Title: Peace activism / by Virginia Loh-Hagan.
Description: Ann Arbor, Michigan : Cherry Lake Publishing, 2021. | Series:
   Stand up, speak out | Includes index.
Identifiers: LCCN 2021005003 (print) | LCCN 2021005004 (ebook) | ISBN
   9781534187573 (hardcover) | ISBN 9781534188976 (paperback) | ISBN
   9781534190375 (pdf) | ISBN 9781534191778 (ebook)
Subjects: LCSH: Peace movements–Juvenile literature. | Pacifists–Juvenile
   literature.
Classification: LCC JZ5574 .L64 2021 (print) | LCC JZ5574 (ebook) | DDC
   303.6/6–dc23
LC record available at https://lccn.loc.gov/2021005003
LC ebook record available at https://lccn.loc.gov/2021005004

Printed in the United States of America
Corporate Graphics

About the Author:

Dr. Virginia Loh-Hagan is an author, university professor, and former classroom teacher. She's currently the Director of the Asian Pacific Islander Desi American Resource Center at San Diego State University. She has stayed at the Fairmont Queen Elizabeth Hotel, which was the location of one of John Lennon's bed-in protests. She lives in San Diego with her very tall husband and very naughty dogs.

TABLE OF CONTENTS

Activists often work as a group.
They have power in numbers.

WHAT IS PEACE ACTIVISM?

Everyone has the power to make our world a better place. A person just has to act. **Activists** fight for change. They fight for their beliefs. They see unfair things. They want to correct wrongs. They want **justice**. Justice is upholding what is right. Activists help others. They serve people and communities.

There are many problems in the world. Activists seek to solve these problems. They learn all they can. They raise awareness. They take action. They inspire others to act.

Activists care very deeply about their **causes**. Causes are principles, aims, or movements. They give rise to activism.

Many activists feel strongly about peace. Peace activists fight for human rights. They want to live freely. They want all people to be treated fairly. They want all people to have their basic needs met. They want to end **conflicts**. Conflicts are fights or battles.

Peace activists speak out. They rise up. They resist. They protest. They do these things in non-violent ways. They don't use force. They avoid hurting others.

In this book, we share examples of peace issues and actions. We also share tips for how to engage. Your activist journey starts here!

The goals of peace movements are justice and freedom.

GET STARTED

Community service is about helping others. It's about creating a kinder world. Activism goes beyond service. It's about making a fairer and more just world. It involves acting and fighting for change. Choose to be an activist!

○ **Focus on your cause!** In addition to the topics covered in this book, there are many others. Other examples include fighting for democracy and ending violence against women.

○ **Do your research!** Learn all you can about the cause. Learn about the history. Learn from other activists.

○ **Make a plan!** Get organized.

○ **Make it happen!** Act! There are many ways to act. Activists write letters. They write petitions. They protest. They march in the streets. They perform art to make people aware. They post to social media. They fight to change laws. They organize sit-in events. They participate in demonstrations and strikes. During strikes, people protest by refusing to do something, such as work.

Muhammed Ali made speeches against the Vietnam War.

CHAPTER 1

STOP ALL WARS

Groups go to war when they can't solve problems. Many wars have been fought in human history. People fight over land. They fight over religion. Peace activists are **anti-war**. Anti-war means against wars. **Pacifists** don't see the point of war. They don't use guns or weapons.

Muhammad Ali was a boxer. He refused to fight in the Vietnam War. He was a **conscientious objector**. Conscientious objectors don't fight in wars due to their religious or political beliefs. Ali was treated like a criminal. His boxing awards were taken away. His was sentenced to jail. He went to court and won. He inspired others. Activists fight for the right for people to object to military service.

GET INSPIRED

BY PIONEERS IN PEACE ACTIVISM!

○ **Jane Addams** won the Nobel Peace Prize in 1931. She was the first woman to do so. Addams created a community center. She provided services and job training to people. During World War I, she promoted world peace. She protested the United States fighting in the war. She was a pacifist. She led the Women's Peace Party. She went to warring countries. She gave speeches about peace.

○ **Mahatma Gandhi** was from India. He fought for peace. He helped Indian people gain independence from Britain. He promoted non-violent protests. He inspired many other leaders. He marched 241 miles (388 kilometers). He hosted hunger strikes. He said, "There are many causes that I am prepared to die for but no causes that I am prepared to kill for."

Activists want tax dollars to be used for public services instead of war.

Activists protest against wars. On February 15, 2003, activists gathered around the world. The largest anti-war rally was in Rome, Italy. It's listed in the *Guinness World Records*. More than 3 million people showed up. These activists opposed the Iraq War. They marched. They sang. They danced. Their signs read, "No to war."

Code Pink is led by women. They seek to end U.S. wars. They use art and street theater to show resistance. They also wear pink. Medea Benjamin is one of the founders.

One in six children around the world live in areas affected by wars.

In 2013, she wrote a book against **drones**. Drones are flying robots. They're used to bomb places in the Middle East. Code Pink aims to stop the drone wars.

Stand Up, Speak Out

In some countries, children are forced to fight in wars. They're known as child soldiers. They're used as spies and fighters. Activists want to ban children from being used in wars. You can help!

> Participate in Red Hand Day on February 12. This is also known as International Day against the Use of Child Soldiers. Collect red handprints and post on social media.

> Host workshops. Teach others about the issues with child soldiers. Show how we all suffer when children suffer.

> Host events to raise funds. Send money to activist groups that rescue child soldiers.

Nuclear fallout is what is left over from a bomb explosion. It can make people very sick.

CHAPTER 2

PROTEST AGAINST NUCLEAR WARFARE

Some countries have **nuclear** weapons. They say these weapons protect safety. They say the weapons secure peace. Nuclear weapons are powerful bombs. They release a lot of energy. They can destroy a city. They can kill many people. Activists want to get rid of nuclear weapons. They don't think nuclear weapons are needed.

Nuclear war would be dangerous. It would end life on Earth. In 2017, countries around the world signed an agreement known as a **treaty**. It's called the Treaty on the **Prohibition** of Nuclear Weapons. Prohibition means ban. ICAN helped create the treaty. ICAN is the International **Campaign** to **Abolish** Nuclear Weapons. Campaign means a course of action. Abolish means to end.

GET INSPIRED

BY LEGAL VICTORIES

○ Mary Beth Tinker was 13 years old in 1965 when she heard about the Vietnam War. She and her friends wanted to protest the war. They wore black armbands to school. School officials banned this. Tinker and her friends fought back. They went to court. They fought for their right to free speech. In 1969, the Supreme Court ruled in her favor. They said, "It can hardly be argued that either students or teachers shed their constitutional rights to freedom of speech or expression at the schoolhouse gate."

○ In 2002, the International Criminal Court (ICC) was created. They keep the peace. They investigate and punish people accused of war crimes. They want to stop these crimes from happening again. The Court is in the Netherlands at the Hague. The Hague is known as the "international city of peace and justice." More than 120 countries are ICC members. The United States in not an ICC member.

ICAN educates people on the dangers of nuclear weapons. They started the "Don't Bank on the Bomb" campaign. They **boycott** companies that support nuclear weapons. Boycott means to avoid or not buy something as a protest. They call on countries to sign the treaty.

Anti-nuclear protestors oppose different nuclear technologies. Besides the possibility of nuclear war,

There are more than 13,000 nuclear warheads in the world. Russia and the United States have the most.

they worry about how nuclear power could impact people and the environment. Since 2011, activists in India have fought against the building of a nuclear power plant. They call themselves the People's Movement Against Nuclear Energy. They host hunger strikes, meaning they refuse to eat as a protest. They block roads to stop trucks from coming in. They host rallies. They host public meetings in villages. They want a peaceful future.

● The United States used nuclear weapons in 1945. They bombed Japan during World War II.

Stand Up, Speak Out

The U.S. president decides when to use a nuclear weapon. Activists want to support a "No First Use" policy. This policy would stop the president from starting a nuclear war. You can help!

> Learn more about the "No First Use" policy. This policy means we don't use nuclear weapons first. We only use them in response if we are attacked by another nuclear weapon.

> Teach others about the dangers of nuclear weapons. Tell them to support the "No First Use" policy. Join together to contact politicians.

> Write to politicians. Ask them to stop spending money on nuclear weapons.

The UN main office is in New York City. It is the site of many protests.

CHAPTER 3

FIGHT FOR WORLD PEACE

World peace would end all wars. People around the world want to be free of violence. They want to feel safe.

In 1945, World War II ended. The world was a mess. People wanted peace. They wanted to stop future world wars. More than 50 countries met in San Francisco. They formed the United Nations (UN). This group maintains international world peace and security. It protects human rights and provides aid. It fights against nuclear weapons. It clears landmines. Today, 193 countries are in the UN.

Tegla Loroupe is from Kenya in Africa. Loroupe holds **marathon** world records. Marathons are long-distance running races. Loroupe believes sports can

GET IN THE KNOW

KNOW THE HISTORY

○ **1815** The New York Peace Society was the first peace society in the United States. They hosted meetings and sent out newsletters. They described the horrors of war.

○ **1863** Henri Dunant was a Swiss activist. He saw the effects of war. He was inspired to form the Red Cross. The Red Cross is an international peace group. It protects human life and health. It provides relief and eases human suffering.

○ **1916** The Women's Peace Crusade was formed. Its members wanted to end World War I. The movement started in Glasgow, Scotland. It spread across Britain.

○ **1933** The Co-operative Women's Guild adopted the white poppy as a symbol of peace. The Guild was established in 1833. It was made up of British women activists. The Guild ended in 2016.

○ **1982** The largest anti-nuclear protest took place in New York City. Buses of people came in from all over the country. More than 1 million people participated.

● John Lennon wrote "Give Peace A Chance" in Montreal, Canada. The song is used in many peace protests.

create peace. In 2003, she started a peace race. Rival African tribes would compete and race each other. In the end, it helped bring people together.

John Lennon was a famous singer. He was a member of the Beatles. He wrote songs about peace. He and his wife, Yoko Ono, hosted bed-in events for world peace. These events were in Amsterdam, Netherlands, and in Montreal, Canada. Lennon and Ono stayed in bed for a week. They let reporters come into their rooms. They filmed their bed-in.

Songs are part of art. Art can be activism. It's called artivism.

Stand Up, Speak Out

Protest songs are used at protests. They have messages. They unite people. They serve as a rallying cry. Activists want to raise awareness about their causes. You can help!

> Celebrate the International Day of Peace on September 21. Host a world peace sing-in event. Gather your friends in one place to sing protest songs.

> Host discussions about protest songs. Talk about the history and message of the songs.

> Think about a cause that's important to you. Write a song about it. Perform it. Share it on social media.

Order Here

The pay it forward concept has been featured in books and movies.

CHAPTER 4

PAY IT FORWARD

When someone does something for you, pass it on. Do something kind for someone else. This is what "pay it forward" means. Peace is founded on kindness. A **random** act of kindness is when someone does something nice just to be nice. Random means without a plan.

In 2020, a pay it forward movement happened in Minnesota. It lasted for 2.5 days. It started with a man who paid for the order of the car behind him at a Dairy Queen drive-through. That person paid for someone else's order. In total, over 900 people paid for someone else's order.

Lizzie Velasquez is an anti-bullying activist. In 2006, she saw a video of the "World's Ugliest Woman."

GET INVOLVED

There are several groups working for peace. Connect with them to get more involved.

- **Kids for Peace** empowers youth. They create peace though global friendships. They create peace through acts of kindness. They send "Peace Packs" to other children around the world. These packs are filled with school supplies, toys, and a note.

- **The Peace Corps** is a volunteer group. Volunteers are people who work for free. The Peace Corps provides help around the world. Volunteers work abroad. They do various peace projects.

- **Peace First** supports young people to lead social change in their communities. They provide training and mentors. They provide money for projects. They host summits, which are large meetings.

- **The United Network of Young People** seeks to increase the role of young people in building world peace. The group wants to shape laws and policies. They have more than 100 member groups.

BE kind to every kind

She realized the video was about her. She was 17 years old at the time. She has a rare disease. She can't gain weight. Velasquez spoke out against bullying. She made speeches. She wrote books. She thinks people should dare to be kind. She said, "Even if you look a little unusual, you're a member of the human race."

● Many activists have started kindness movements.

People around the world are bullied. They're bullied because they're different. Peace starts with kindness.

World Kindness Day is November 13.

Stand Up, Speak Out

Pay It Forward Day is on April 28. It's celebrated around the world. It encourages people to be kind. It inspires people to start a chain of kindness. Activists want to promote peace. We can practice peace every day. We can practice peace all year long. You can help!

➤ Be alert. Watch for chances to help others. Act when not asked. Reach out without expecting anything in return.

➤ Do something nice for someone you don't know.

➤ Spread the word. Spread kindness. Do a good deed. If someone thanks you, ask them to pay it forward.

GLOSSARY

abolish (uh-BOL-ish) to end or stop completely

activists (AK-tih-vists) people who fight for political or social change

anti-war (an-TEE-wor) being against war

boycott (BOI-kot) to refuse to buy something or take part in something as a protest to force change

campaign (kam-PAYN) an organized course of action

causes (KAWZ-es) the reasons for activism

conflicts (KON-flicts) disagreements between people, such as fights or battles

conscientious objector (kon-shee-EN-shuhss uhb-JEK-tuhr) a person who refuses to serve in the military because of religious or political beliefs

drones (DRONES) flying robots

justice (JUHSS-tiss) the upholding of what is fair and right

marathon (MAR-uh-thon) a long-distance running race

nuclear (NOO-klee-ur) being a weapon whose destructive power comes from a powerful, dangerous explosion

pacifists (PASS-uh-fists) people who don't view war as a justifiable means to end conflict

prohibition (proh-uh-BIH-shuhn) ban

random (RAN-duhm) without a plan, done without thinking

strikes (STRYKES) organized protests where people refuse to do something

treaty (TREE-tee) an agreement

LEARN MORE!

Krishnaswami, Uma. *Threads of Peace: How Mohandas Gandhi and Martin Luther King Jr. Changed the World.* New York, NY: Atheneum/Caitlyn Dlouhy Books, 2021.

Paul, Caroline, and Lauren Tamaki (illust.). *You Are Mighty: A Guide to Changing the World.* New York, NY: Bloomsbury Children's Books, 2018.

Zabinski, Tanya. *Peace, Love, Action! Everyday Acts of Goodness from A to Z.* Berkley, CA: Plum Blossom Books, 2019.

INDEX